I'VE SEEN
HEAVEN
EXPERIENCING THE DIVINE

ISBN 978-1-61795-331-6

Published by Worthy Inspired, a division of Worthy Media, Inc.,
134 Franklin Road, Suite 200, Brentwood, Tennessee 37027.

Scripture references marked KJV are from the Holy Bible, King James Version.

Scripture references marked NKJV are from the Holy Bible, New King James Version. Copyright © 1982 by Thomas Nelson, Inc. Used by permission.

Scripture references marked HCSB are from the Holman Christian Standard Bible™. Copyright © 1999, 2000, 2001 by Holman Bible Publishers. Used by permission.

Scripture references marked NIV are from the Holy Bible, New International Version®, NIV® Copyright © 1973, 1978, 1984, 2011 by Biblica, Inc.® Used by permission. All rights reserved worldwide.

Scripture references marked NLT are from the Holy Bible, New Living Translation. Copyright © 1996 Tyndale Charitable Trust. Used by permission of Tyndale House Publishers.

Scripture references marked ESV are from the Holy Bible, English Standard Version. The Holy Bible, English Standard Version. Copyright © 2001 by Crossway Bibles, a division of Good News Publishers.

Scripture references marked MSG are from the Message. Copyright © 1993, 1994, 1995, 1996, 2000, 2001, 2002. Used by permission of NavPress Publishing Group.

Scripture references marked GNT are from the Holy Bible, Good News Translation. Copyright © 1992 by American Bible Society

Scripture references marked TLB are from the Holy Bible, The Living Bible copyright © 1971 by Tyndale House Foundation. Used by permission of Tyndale House Publishers Inc., Carol Stream, Illinois 60188. All rights reserved.

Cover Design by Kim Russell/Wahoo Designs
Page Layout by Bart Dawson

Printed in the United States of America

1 2 3 4 5—LBM—18 17 16 15 14

I'VE SEEN HEAVEN

EXPERIENCING THE DIVINE

BOB DEMOSS

NEW YORK TIMES BESTSELLING AUTHOR

DEDICATION

∾

For my son, Daniel Philip DeMoss.

I love your tender warrior heart and your penetrating

questions about Jesus and Heaven.

Always keep your gaze fixed upon His Kingdom.

TABLE OF CONTENTS

INTRODUCTION

In December 2013, my friend Mark Gilroy at Worthy Publishing approached me with the idea for this book. Mark caught me during a time when I had just left my role as an associate publisher at HarperCollins Christian Publishing. Intrigued by the topic of Heaven, I agreed to do the book. That's when I made an embarrassing discovery, namely, I knew less about Heaven than I originally thought. Talk about ironic. I've been living my life as a follower of Jesus from my youth. My heart's desire has been, and continues to be, spending eternity with Him.

Everything else on earth—every endeavor I undertake—pales by comparison.

But an hour into the writing I was overwhelmed with the reality that my view of Heaven was pretty anemic. Worse, I quickly learned that my view of Heaven was academic, sterile, and definitely incomplete. With my wife's blessing and the prayers and support of my children, I packed my bags for a two-week writing retreat to jumpstart the book and, most importantly, to reacquaint my heart with what the Bible has to say about my eternal home.

I traveled to a scenic lakefront location in Alabama, to a cottage owned by my friend Eddie DeGarmo and his wife Susan. Their retreat provided the perfect distraction-free environment to pray, read, think, and write. Digging into what the Bible says about Heaven was Job #1. And, I immersed myself in what a number of biblical scholars and trusted Bible teachers had written on the subject.

I also read testimony after testimony from pastors, truck drivers, housewives, doctors, real estate brokers, athletes, cops, and businessmen, indeed people from all walks of life and from around the world, both the very young and the very old, the highly educated and the unschooled, who reported their visit to Heaven during what's popularly known as a "near-death experience" (NDE). In each of these stories, the refrain was the same: *I've seen Heaven and I didn't want to leave.*

One bestselling pastor, however, blasts these visions of Heaven as nothing more than "imaginary tales" that no "reputable evangelical publisher would have given a second glance to just twenty years ago" but that booksellers are happily selling "books filled with false visions of the afterlife."[1] He takes issue with the "unbiblical picture of Heaven from these tall tales . . . There is no reason to believe anyone who claims to have gone to Heaven and returned."[2]

What are we to make of this? Are these testimonies distractions from the devil designed to mislead believers? Or, are they glimpses of Heaven from God to nudge us into a deeper exploration of eternal life? Mark Galli, editor of *Christianity Today*, says, "In most cases, people who have had near-Heaven experiences return to earth and give themselves in love and service of others. If the Devil is inspiring such godly work, he's confused about his job description."[3]

Personally, I'm not quick to write off firsthand accounts by those who have experienced the Divine. Why? As you'll see in chapter two, four years ago my own brother died and was clinically dead for three minutes—and then returned to life. Suffice it to say that his story wasn't an "imaginary tale." I was powerfully and profoundly impacted by that family crisis. What's more, the Bible tells us, "I will pour out my Spirit on all people. Your sons and daughters will prophesy, your old men will dream dreams, your young men will see visions" (Joel 2:28 NIV). This Old Testament prophecy that "your young men will see visions, your old men will dream dreams" was repeated by Peter in Acts 2:17.

Dreams and visions of what?

It's reasonable to believe Heaven would be on the short list of subjects.

Why, then, would we be uncomfortable when our young men, like Todd Burpo's son Colton, have a Heavenly vision? I believe there's wisdom in listening and learning what we can. At the same time, you and I should weigh any such testimony about Heaven through the lens of Scripture. As the Apostle John has said, "Dear friends, do not believe every spirit, but test the spirits to see whether they are from God, because many false prophets have gone out into the world" (1 John 4:1 NIV).

That said, this book isn't intended to be a comprehensive exposé or the definitive work on Heaven. Think of these pages more like a "free sample" that you get in the food court at the mall—it's an initial taste of what awaits those who hunger to know more about the Celestial City. If you'd like to take a deeper dive after reading this little book, I'd encourage you to continue your exploration with three excellent resources, namely, Randy Alcorn's *HEAVEN*, Joni Eareckson Tada's *Heaven: Your Real Home*, and Billy Graham's *Angels*.

If you're ready to catch a vision of your own—a vision of just how incredible Jesus is and how you'll want to spend eternity with Him, then read on. Set aside your ever-present "To Do" list, find a quiet spot away from the static of your daily routine, and join me on this grand tour of your new home. I'm convinced a picture will emerge that what God has prepared for us in His presence is a place more joyful, more glorious, and more dazzling than anything you and I can imagine.

You won't want to miss it!

"When you speak of Heaven, . . .
let your face light up, let it be irradiated
with a heavenly gleam, let your eyes shine
with reflected glory.
But when you speak of Hell—well,
then your ordinary face will do."

—

Charles Spurgeon[4]

"On that day the Lord their God will rescue
his people . . . They will sparkle in his land
like jewels in a crown. How wonderful
and beautiful they will be!"

—

Zechariah 9:16–17a (NLT)

Chapter 1

HEAVEN IS A PLACE OF BOUNDLESS BEAUTY

*T*he first time I saw Heaven I was nine years old.

Don't get me wrong. I didn't have an out-of-body episode. I wasn't in a coma. I didn't drown or get hit by a car and die for several minutes before rejoining this world. That didn't prevent me from having a visceral experience, one in which I felt as if I were standing at the glittering gates to the Celestial City.

I distinctly recall sitting, feet barely touching the floor, at our kitchen table when I saw Heaven. The aroma of Mom's dinner lingered in the air as my dad began to read the book of Revelation from the *Good News for Modern Man.* I was captivated by the description of Jesus with His eyes like "blazing fire" and His face like the "sun shining in all of its brilliance," of the mighty angels with legs like "fiery pillars," and of the New Jerusalem.

I marveled as Dad read: "The wall was made of jasper, and the city itself was made of pure gold, clear as glass. The foundation stones of the city wall were adorned with all kinds of precious stones" (21:18–19). I remember thinking,

"Pure gold that you can actually see through? That'd be more amazing than Mom's shiny 24-karat-gold medallion her mom brought her from Greece."

Keep in mind, I was a typical nine-year-old boy who pocketed fools gold, colorful marbles, and the occasional piece of quartz. I had a serious stash of shiny rocks in a shoebox under my bed. But Dad blew me away when, in addition to the see-through gold, he said this glorious city was *covered* with a vast collection of gemstones that I'd never heard of before—jewels like sapphire, agate, emerald, onyx, carnelian, beryl, topaz, chalcedony, turquoise, and amethyst. That *had* to be way more beautiful than all of the fancy gems in the jewelry case at Sears.

Then Dad read: "The twelve gates were twelve pearls; each gate was made from a single pearl. The street of the city was of pure gold, transparent as glass" (21:21). *Whoa!* A single pearl in Heaven was so large, just one was needed to make an entire city gate out of it? I figured that pearl had to be as enormous as our whole house because clearly the gate had to be at least as massive as the one they used in *The Wizard of Oz*.

Best of all, Dad explained this beautiful city was the place all Christians would be moving to one day to live with Jesus. He called it our "eternal destiny" and our "inheritance" as believers. Deeply impacted by these descriptions, the second we were dismissed from the dinner table, I dashed down the steps to our playroom. I zoomed to my pile of Flintstones Building Boulders—white interlocking Styrofoam blocks that, much like Legos only a hundred times larger, could be snapped together to make forts, towers, and playhouses—and I got busy building my replica of the New Jerusalem.

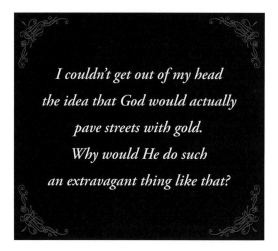

I couldn't get out of my head the idea that God would actually pave streets with gold. Why would He do such an extravagant thing like that?

Alas, my shabby Flintstone Castle was a far cry from the splendor of the Heavenly City I envisioned. Didn't matter. In my own childlike way, I was engaging with what the Bible taught about Heaven. As I went to bed, I couldn't get out of my head the idea that God would actually pave streets with gold. Why would He do such an extravagant thing like that? How could anyone afford to do that? For weeks and months I had Heaven constantly on my mind. I'd pepper my parents with all manner of questions, not the least of which was, "Why would anyone *not* want to go to such a beautiful place like Heaven?"

Over the years, I confess my passion for Heaven dimmed as the clouds, precipitated by the busyness of life, blocked my view. You know the drill. We get so preoccupied raising a family, holding down a job, paying bills, shuttling kids to their activities, repairing stuff . . . attending stuff . . . doing stuff, we forget "to gaze on the beauty of the Lord and to seek him in his temple" (Psalm 27:4 NIV).

How about you? Have you had a childlike "ah ha" moment when you glimpsed Heaven? Was there a time when you realized that God is preparing a place for us more beautiful and glorious than anything we can experience in this life? Maybe, like me, you've allowed the world to crowd out the wonder and delightful anticipation of our eternal home. Here's the good news. Our forgetfulness "to gaze on the beauty of the Lord" doesn't alter the fact that He continues to prepare a home for His children, one that will exceed our wildest imaginations. Take heart! The day is come when, as Zechariah writes, you and I "will sparkle in his land like jewels in a crown."

"You will not be in Heaven two seconds before
you cry out, 'Why did I place so much importance
on things that were so temporary?
What was I thinking? Why did I waste so much time,
energy and concern on what wasn't going to last?'"

—

Rick Warren[5]

"Lord, remind me how brief my time on earth will be.
Remind me that my days are numbered—
how fleeting my life is."

—

Psalm 39:4 (NLT)

Chapter 2

HEAVEN IS A PLACE ONE HEARTBEAT AWAY

*O*n February 11, 2008, my sister Becky called from Philadelphia. Her words were uncharacteristically clipped, devoid of her usual effervescence and warmth. Half awake, I blinked at the clock. Not quite 6 a.m. in Nashville. The urgency in her voice hit me like a glass of cold water in the face: "They've taken Steve by ambulance to Abington Hospital." Before I could ask "Why?" she added, "The right side of his face is numb. They're running tests right now. Might be a blood clot—maybe a stroke. *Pray*."

I did. We all did.

At age 49, Steve, a professional painter, was in excellent physical shape. His daily routine included a four-mile jog. This made his sudden medical crisis completely unexpected and initially difficult to diagnose. The doctors ran a battery of tests. About two hours later, Becky called again. "They did a CAT scan. Steve didn't have a stroke—he has a torn aortic valve. They're rushing him into surgery . . . it's likely he won't make it. If you can, you better take the next plane."

Won't make it? Why not?

Evidently, reconstructing the aorta is a rare procedure with a high mortality rate—my brother had a mere 4 percent chance of surviving the surgery. I raced to the airport in time to catch a nonstop flight to Philly. Gazing out the window as we took flight, a flood of memories flashed through my mind. As boys, we shared bunk beds. As young men, I was so proud of his courageous mission work in Uganda that began in the chaos left behind by the brutal madman Idi Amin. As adults, we brainstormed many "million-dollar ideas"—none of which have panned out, but dreaming them up was the fun part.

From my birds-eye view as the plane leveled off at 36,000 feet, I was awestruck as the heavens put on the most glorious display I've ever seen in all of my travels—and I've flown a lot. Thick clouds formed puffy, quilt-like blankets neatly above and below the plane as a sea of crystal blue sky stretched across the middle third of the skyline. A brilliant golden sun, lingering at the edge of the horizon, topped this celestial layer cake of beauty. That's when the words of King David came to mind:

"The heavens declare the glory of God; the skies proclaim the work of his hands" (Psalm 19:1 NIV).

In that sacred moment as I communed in my heart with the Lord, I couldn't shake the feeling that Steve was gone. I felt he was already in Heaven. True, this old world with its potholes, sickness, rust, scandals, disasters, and wars is no match for the perfection, peace, and glory of Heaven, or the joy of being in the eternal presence of our loving Heavenly Father. Still, tears stung the edges of my eyes at the thought I was going to be too late to tell my younger brother how much I loved him.

"*Please*, Jesus," I whispered. "Please, not now . . . I know it's selfish, but I don't want to lose my brother."

I continued to pray in spite of my gut feeling that he had died.

Steve's surgery was in progress so I'd know soon enough whether or not the Lord would grant our prayers on his behalf. Upon landing in Philly, as the plane taxied to the gate, my cell phone exploded with updates from various family members. I figured there must be bad news since only a couple of hours had passed instead of the anticipated six-to-eight-hour surgery. Listening to the messages, I was overjoyed. The operation was a success. Granted, Steve was still in the intensive care unit, but his vital signs looked promising.

Steve remained in ICU for the better part of a week where his doctors kept him in an induced coma to allow his body to heal. Meanwhile, my family, joined by friends from around the world, continued to pray over Steve. After all, as the doctor explained, at one point my brother actually *did* die during the surgery. Turns out what I was feeling in my heart while looking out the airplane window was true. He *was* gone. Steve had no pulse. No brainwave activity. His heart monitor displayed only a razor-thin flatline.

Steve was clinically dead.

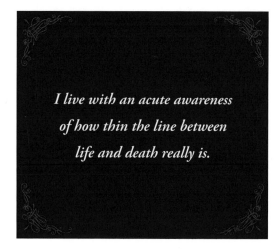

I live with an acute awareness of how thin the line between life and death really is.

In the words of celebrated neurologist Dr. Eben Alexander who had his own NDE, "When your brain is absent, you are absent, too . . . If you don't have a working brain, you can't be conscious. This is because the brain is the machine that produces consciousness in the first place. When the machine breaks down, consciousness stops." To further illustrate his point, Dr. Alexander added, "Pull the plug and the TV goes dead. The show is over, no matter how much you might have been enjoying it."[6]

But the "show" wasn't entirely over for Steve. Why?

One of Steve's nurses, Barb Oelschlegel, a dear friend from church, later commented, "I saw angels on the ceiling of the operating room . . . the angels are in the room with him so things are going well." Although Steve's doctors couldn't explain it, they watched his EKG monitor dance back to life after three long minutes of zero brain activity. Where did he go? What did he see? Was there a "white light"? Did his life flash before his eyes? Did he recognize any of our family who had previously died?

Did he see Jesus?

We had to wait for several days for those answers.

Candidly, his description of what he saw surprised me. While Steve joins the others who can say "I've seen Heaven," he is not ready to talk about it publically. Perhaps one day Steve will feel comfortable talking about what he witnessed. I respectfully defer to him in such matters. Suffice it to say that his taste of the afterlife was a life-changing experience. He said it best: "I pray it wouldn't take another near-death experience to wake me up to what really matters. I want to love and serve Him each day and not waste the remaining time He gives me on Earth . . . I owe Him a hundred lifetimes!"

As I worked on this book, my brother told me, "Even though I died and came back several years ago, I live with an acute awareness of how thin the line between life and death really is." Indeed, we are just one car accident, one viral infection, one diagnosis away from having our business-as-usual lifestyle thrown out the window. We would do well to heed the words of Peter, a follower of Jesus, who said, "Friends, this world is not your home, so don't make yourselves cozy in it. Don't indulge your ego at the expense of your soul"

(1 Peter 2:11 MSG).

Do you know someone who has recovered from a serious illness and who claims to have seen Heaven or an angelic being? How did you react? Were you skeptical or perhaps curious about the reality of Heaven? Either way, don't lose sight of the larger truth: Jesus has placed a Welcome Home mat by the front door to the mansion He has prepared for you. Since you don't know when your moving day will be (Ecclesiastes 9:12), what choices can you make today that will draw you and your family closer to Jesus while preparing your heart for Heaven?

"We'll be learners forever.
God doesn't want us to stop learning.
What he wants to stop is what
prevents us from learning."

—

Randy Alcorn[7]

"For now we see only a reflection as in a mirror;
then we shall see face to face.
Now I know in part; then I shall know fully,
even as I am fully known."

—

1 Corinthians 13:12 (NIV)

Chapter 3

HEAVEN IS A PLACE OF UNDERSTANDING

We have a rule in our house: There are no dumb questions.

The quickest way to stifle learning is to limit the scope of the inquiry our children may have. Our eight-year-old son Danny, who has no shortage of questions, including who invented Legos and baseball and why some dogs are so mean—recently asked me, "Since Jesus and God are the same person, do they have the same face?" Think about that for a minute.

Do they?

Danny daily exhibits his God-given thirst for knowledge. Indeed, our desire to understand our world compels us to search for the answers to life's mysteries. In a way, life is like a giant scavenger hunt, a game of discovery in which God embedded creation with clues unlocking the DNA of the universe. Perhaps the most complex mystery of all is understanding how human consciousness and the brain, with its estimated 85–100 *billion* neurons, function together. That's been the lifelong quest of Dr. Eben Alexander.

As a man of medical science, Dr. Alexander spent eleven years training to become a neurosurgeon at some of America's most prestigious institutions, including Duke and Harvard. The brain, with its astounding complexity, is a magnificent tribute to God. And yet, Dr. Alexander confesses he wasn't a person of faith: "As much as I'd grown up wanting to believe in God and Heaven and an afterlife, my decades in the rigorous scientific world of academic neurosurgery had profoundly called into question how such things could exist."[8]

Although he had numerous patients describing NDEs, he considered these nothing more than "pure fantasy" on par with tales of the Easter Bunny and Big Foot sightings. The events of November 10, 2008, would change his unbelief. That's when illness struck—a pain so intense Dr. Alexander was roused from a deep sleep. What started out as a puzzling ache rapidly became a debilitating enigma. Within hours, his condition went from bad to worse as his body twisted and jerked about as if shot with a stun gun.

As the ambulance raced to the very hospital where he practiced neurosurgery, delirium set in. His face turned crimson red, his arms flailed uncontrollably. He entered the throws of a full grand mal seizure as the EMTs rushed him inside. His doctors ultimately discovered he had a rare case of *E. coli* bacterial meningitis—a stark diagnosis with just a 10 percent survival rate and a disease that was virtually impossible for him to have.[9]

That's when his world came crashing down.

For seven days, he lay in a deep coma, lifeless as a stone, during which time his brain completely shut down. As he details in his extraordinary bestselling book, *Proof of Heaven*, ". . . my entire neocortex—the outer surface of the brain, the part that makes us human—was shut down. Inoperative. In essence, absent."[10] Adding, "my brain wasn't working improperly—it wasn't working *at all*."[11] After seven days of trying to bring Dr. Alexander back, his medical team had to concede there was nothing left to do but unplug the machines artificially keeping his body tethered to this earth.

With no brain activity, what choice did they have?

In spite of the conspicuous lack of brain functionality, Dr. Alexander saw Heaven. "The place I went was real," he writes. "Real in a way that makes the life we're living here and now completely dreamlike by comparison."[12] Given his craving for knowledge and insight, he was blown away by the "staggering heights of communication and understanding that lie ahead for us all, when each of us leaves the limitations of our physical body and brain behind."[13] Gone are the barriers to learning. He describes the phenomenon this way:

". . . a question would arise in my mind, and the answer would arise at the same time . . . there was no such thing as a question without an accompanying answer. These answers were not simple 'yes' or 'no' fare, either. They were vast conceptual edifices, staggering structures of living thought, as intricate as cities. Ideas so vast they would have taken me lifetimes to find my way around if I had been confined to earthly thought."[14]

How has his view of God changed by this experience? He reflects, God is "completely beyond any of our human attempts at capturing God in words or pictures."[15] Adding, "In my past view, *spiritual* wasn't a word that I would have employed during a scientific conversation. Now I believe it is a word that we cannot afford to leave out." His bottom line? "Each and every one of us is deeply known and cared for by a Creator who cherishes us beyond any ability to comprehend."[16] That resonates with what the Apostle Paul said about Heaven, namely, "Now I know in part; then I shall know fully, even as I am fully known."

All of us have unanswered questions, unresolved issues, and a need for clarity. Maybe you cannot understand how a loving God could allow you to experience the emotional or physical abuse you've secretly endured for years. Perhaps you struggle to comprehend why your prodigal child is unresponsive to your unconditional love. Maybe you're grappling with the betrayal by a business partner or a spouse. You

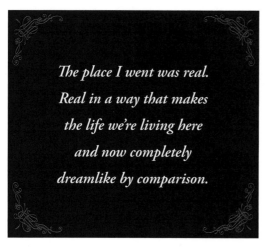

The place I went was real. Real in a way that makes the life we're living here and now completely dreamlike by comparison.

might be wondering how anyone could be so cruel as to walk out on their commitment. Whatever questions you may have in this lifetime, take comfort that Heaven is a place of understanding—where you are known and loved unconditionally by Jesus who, likewise, was betrayed and suffered injustice.

Be encouraged. In Heaven, borrowing a line from the great late radio personality Paul Harvey, you'll know *"the rest of the story."*

"Those whom you laid in the grave with
many tears are in good keeping:
you will yet see them again with joy.
Believe it, think it, rest on it. It is all true."

—

J. C. Ryle[17]

"First, the Christians who have died will rise
from their graves. Then, together with them,
we who are still alive and remain on the earth
will be caught up in the clouds to meet the Lord
in the air. Then we will be with the Lord forever."

—

1 Thessalonians 4:16b–17 (NLT)

Chapter 4

HEAVEN IS
A PLACE OF
REUNIONS

"If you could ask God one question about Heaven, what would it be?"

Hundreds of people responded to that post on my friend's Facebook page. Some of the responses were lighthearted: *"Will I be able to go fishing?"* Some were sobering: *"Father, did I make you proud of the life you gave me on earth?"* Others were deeply moving: *"Will I be loved and accepted by my aborted children?"* But, by far, the most frequently asked question was this:

"Will I be reunited with my family and friends who died before me?"

If that question is on your mind, read on.

During 1989, more than 45,000 died in motor-vehicle-related accidents.[18] Don Piper was one of them . . . at least for 90 minutes. With a driving rain pelting his little red Ford Escort, Don was heading home from a pastors conference in Texas. At 11:45 a.m. disaster in the form of an on-coming truck struck. Literally. Swerving into his lane, traveling more than 60 miles-per-hour, the massive 18-wheeler slammed head-on into Don's pint-size car and then crushed his vehicle under its wheels as if the hatchback were just a pebble.

Inside the crumpled car, Don's mangled body had been impaled by his steering wheel. His left leg was mashed between the dash and his seat. Shards of glass like knives stabbed his head, face, and chest. Paramedics were summoned to the scene. After several attempts to find a pulse, and unable to detect any signs of life, Don was declared dead. There was nothing left for the EMTs to do—except to place a tarp over the collapsed roof sparing onlookers from the grotesque view.

That was the happiest day of Don's life on Earth. Why?

One minute Don was navigating his car across a bridge in a rainstorm. The next moment he found himself standing in Heaven experiencing a joy so complete, so delightful, it "pulsated" through his body—a virtual "first class buffet for the senses."[19] In his bestseller, *90 Minutes in Heaven*, Don describes being greeted by a "celestial welcoming committee" made up of family and friends who had died during his lifetime. With outstretched arms, his grandfather called him by his nickname "Donnie." Don writes, "He looked exactly as I remembered him, with his shock of white hair and what I called a big banana nose . . . he was once again the robust, strong grandfather I had remembered as a child."[20]

One by one, the joyous well-wishers in Heaven embraced Don, laughing and radiating with a peacefulness he had never experienced before. He met his great-grandfather and great-grandmother, one of his best childhood friends, a classmate who had drowned, and several teachers from high school, among others. Don observed that the "people I encountered were the same age they had been the last time I had seen them—except that all the ravages of living on earth had vanished."[21]

While Don was celebrating with his loved ones in Heaven, back on earth Dick Onerecker, a guest speaker who had attended the same conference as Don, who was traveling the same road as Don, found himself in a traffic jam caused by the wreckage. Prompted by the Holy Spirit, Dick approached the police on the scene with an offer to pray for the injured. The officer indicated the person in the red car under the tarp was deceased. Dick didn't know who the dead passenger was, yet he felt compelled to pray for him or her. Against the advice of the police, Dick approached the car, lifted the tarp, and crawled through the hatchback.

Dick had been a medic in Vietnam so he was accustomed to bloody injuries—although what he saw of the lifeless corpse shocked him. He felt for a pulse and, finding none, began to pray harder than he'd ever prayed before. That's when the miraculous happened. Ninety minutes after Don had been pronounced dead, he returned to his shattered earthly body.

The news that the dead man lived electrified the emergency personnel on the scene. Using the Jaws of Life, they extracted Don from the deathtrap—which was the first step on the road to a very long recovery. Don needed 34 surgeries and spent 105 days in the hospital healing both physically and emotionally. When

He was once again the robust, strong grandfather I had remembered as a child.

asked about his experience in Heaven during those 90 minutes, Don writes, "Heaven was many things, but without a doubt, it was the greatest family reunion of all."[22]

The *greatest family reunion* sure has a nice ring to it, doesn't it?

Let's set aside Don's experience for a moment.

Are you saddened today at the loss of a cherished Christian friend? Is your heart grieving the loss of your spouse, a child, your parents, or other members of your family? Do you have doubts about the reality of rejoining your beloved in Heaven? Listen to what Jesus told His followers: "I say to you that many will come from the east and the west, and will take their places at the feast with Abraham, Isaac and Jacob in the kingdom of heaven" (Matthew 8:11 NIV). Ponder Jesus' declaration with me for a moment. How can believers participate in His promised heavenly banquet without a reunion of those who once walked the earth? Furthermore, what kind of a reunion would it be if we cannot recognize one another?

This is how Paul encouraged the believers of his day on this question of being reunited with those who've gone to glory before us: "And now, dear brothers and sisters, we want you to know what will happen to the believers who have died so you will not grieve like people who have no hope . . . when Jesus returns, God will bring back with him the believers who have died" (1 Thessalonians 4:13–14 NLT).

So be encouraged. The table is being set. The banquet hall is being decorated.

It's a feast fit for a King and all of His people.

This *will* be the grandest family reunion ever.

"Music is God's gift to man,
the only art of Heaven given to earth,
the only art of earth we take to Heaven."

—

Walter Savage Landor[23]

"The Lord will save me, and we will sing
with stringed instruments
all the days of our lives in the temple of the Lord."

—

Isaiah 38:20 (NIV)

Chapter 5

HEAVEN IS
A PLACE OF MUSIC
AND WORSHIP

*W*hat do you do when you're driving your car and a favorite song comes on the radio? If you're like me, you turn up the volume—and lower the windows if it's a sunny day. After all, music has a powerful way of connecting with us on an emotional and spiritual level. Stylistically, my tastes are all over the map—classic rock, classical, and, of late, country music. Regarding the traditional hymns I learned as a child, "How Great Thou Art," "Rock of Ages," and "It Is Well with My Soul" top my list. As an adult, I enjoy contemporary worship songs such as "How Great Is Our God," "Mighty to Save" or "Blessed Be Your Name."

No doubt you have a long list of personal favorites, too.

Which begs a question: *Will there be music in Heaven?*

John's vision of Heaven recorded in Revelation holds the answer. For starters, John, the beloved disciple of Jesus, describes this astounding scene within the throne room of God: "Then I looked and heard the voice of many angels, numbering thousands upon thousands, and *ten thousand* times *ten thousand*.

They encircled the throne and the living creatures and the elders" (Revelation 5:11a NIV; emphasis added).

When John speaks of angels numbering *"ten thousand* times *ten thousand"* he's using the largest number available to him based upon the ancient Greek mathematical system, namely, a hundred million angels. Some perspective on that figure is in order. The Indianapolis Motor Speedway is the largest racing venue in the world, seating 400,000 people. Picture 250 of these stadiums sitting side-by-side—which would cover the entire city of Chicago. Now, picture them jammed with a capacity crowd of angels.

That's what 100 million looks like. If you're like me, I have difficulty comprehending such a stunning sight—angels by the millions, in all of their brilliance, swirling around God's throne. Keep in mind that figure is likely an understatement. Why? The English equivalence of John's *"ten thousand* times *ten thousand"* phrase is "infinity." In other words, John is saying he saw *countless* angels circling God's throne.

What were these celestial beings doing? Singing and worshiping the Lord in song. John writes, "And they sang in a mighty chorus: 'Worthy is the Lamb who was slaughtered—to receive power and wisdom and strength and honor and glory and blessing" (5:12 NLT). He goes on to describe how "every creature in heaven and on earth and under the earth and in the sea" (v. 13a NLT) began to sing, too.

Without question, the most stirring, breathtaking, emotionally evocative piece of music ever sung on earth is an inadequate foretaste of what we'll hear in Heaven when our voices unite with the angelic chorus. The contrast between music in this world and in Heaven would be as drastic as a novice plunking out "Chopsticks" followed by a performance by Chopin in a piano recital.

Don Piper commented on the unforgettable music and worship he encountered. Once again from his *90 Minutes in Heaven* testimony, Piper says his most vivid memories are of the things he heard:

"The praise was unending, but the most remarkable thing to me was that hundreds of songs were being sung at the same time—all of them worshiping God . . . I heard them from every direction and realized that each voice praised God . . . Every sound blended, and each voice or instrument enhanced the others."[24]

Can you imagine what a thrill that will be for us to one day witness? I can picture Mozart, Handel, and Beethoven clapping their hands in delight at the musical feast for their ears, not to mention the inspiration coursing through their gifted imaginations. And, there would be plenty of room for the new music they might dream up. According to Piper, a wide range of musical styles was present in Heaven. He adds:

"Many of the old hymns and choruses I had sung at various times in my life were part of the music—along with hundreds of songs I had never heard before. Hymns of praise, modern-sounding choruses, and ancient chants filled my ears and brought not only a deep peace but the greatest feeling of joy I've ever experienced."[25]

Piper's descriptions would resonate with Jeanette Mitchell-Meadows, a woman who saw Heaven during a nine-hour spinal fusion surgery. She says the music of Heaven "is almost impossible to describe. It is glorious . . . There were musical notes I have never heard on earth. They were so clear and flawless, and the tone was so beautiful."[26] That's also the memory of Alex Malarkey who, at age six, was in a serious car accident that severed his skull from his spine. For two months, Alex hovered between life and death in a coma. That's when Alex saw Heaven. He describes the music as "beautiful" and "nothing like music here. It is perfect!"[27]

I find it fascinating that music played a part during the Savior's time walking upon our soil. If you recall, Jesus sang hymns with His closest companions (Mark 14:26), which demonstrates music is instrumental in both fostering praise to God and fellowship within the community of believers. Pastor and author A.W. Tozer observes, "Without worship, we go about miserable." In other words, benefit of worship is that it takes our eyes off of ourselves and our temporal pursuits and places them on the One worthy of our affections. What's more, when we engage in worship, that's where the authentic transformation of our hearts can take place. As Jack Hayford, pastor and author of the popular worship song "Majesty," has said, "Worship changes the worshiper into the image of the One worshiped."

Do you find yourself singing the blues of late? Are there pressing issues troubling your heart today? Like a thief, has anxiety robbed your joy? If so, when was the last time you allowed the power of music to usher your thirsty soul into God's presence? Maybe it's time to dust off that old guitar sitting in the corner or time to pull a chair up to the piano and enjoy a few private moments having a musical dialogue with Jesus. If you don't know how to play, you can of course listen to any of the fine CDs available or even try learning an instrument and, in turn,

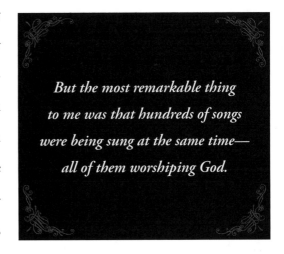

But the most remarkable thing to me was that hundreds of songs were being sung at the same time— all of them worshiping God.

allow music to accomplish what it was ultimately designed to do—transport us into the presence of God.

Where countless angels never stop rejoicing.

Where we will forever delight in the Lord.

"The empire of angels is as vast as God's creation. If you believe the Bible, you will believe in their ministry. They crisscross the Old and New Testaments, being mentioned directly or indirectly nearly three hundred times."

—

Billy Graham[28]

"God will put his angels in charge of you to protect you wherever you go."

—

Psalm 91:11 (GNT)

Chapter 6

HEAVEN IS A PLACE OF ANGELS

*I*n the spring of 2011, world-renowned Cambridge cosmologist Stephen Hawking asserted, "There is no Heaven or afterlife. That is a fairy story for people afraid of the dark."[29] No Heaven? No afterlife? Based upon each of their firsthand experiences, the following individuals would respectfully disagree. I'm referring to Jacob from the Bible, Dr. Mary Neal, and Crystal McVea. Not only would they disagree with Hawking about the reality of Heaven, they all saw angels.

Beginning with Jacob, let's consider their stories and the implications for us.

Remember the biblical account known as "Jacob's Ladder"? Here's a refresher. Isaac and Rebekah had twin boys whose temperaments were as opposite as vinegar is to oil. The firstborn Esau was a hunter, a man of the great outdoors. Bow and arrows, knives and spears were the tools of his trade. Jacob preferred the comforts of home and cooking in the kitchen. Pots, utensils, and an apron were his tools of choice.

The time came for Isaac to give his firstborn the patriarchal blessing. Using a string of lies and deceitful tactics, Jacob double-crossed his brother Esau by successfully stealing Esau's blessing. Enraged, Esau vowed to hunt down and kill Jacob. Learning of this threat, Rebekah urged Jacob to flee until Esau's fury subsided. Jacob, in turn, ran for his life—probably looking over his shoulder the entire way.

As the sun set, Jacob the fugitive was no doubt exhausted and scared out of his wits. He was a stranger in a foreign land. Using a rock as a pillow, he fell asleep. In the midst of this drama, Jacob had an encounter with God in which he saw "a stairway resting on the earth, with its top reaching to heaven, and the angels of God were ascending and descending on it" (Genesis 28:12 NIV). We're then told that Jacob saw the Lord standing at the top of the stairway where He outlined a number of the future events pertaining to Jacob's life (vv. 13–15).

Keep in mind, Jacob didn't have imagery of angels from pop culture to prepare him in any way for what he witnessed. He never heard songs like

"Stairway to Heaven," "Earth Angel," or "Angel Eyes." He never watched TV shows like *Touched by an Angel* or *Highway to Heaven*. Clearly, this encounter with God and the angels and his glimpse of Heaven deeply impacted Jacob.

For starters, he called the place where he slept that night "none other than the house of God; this is the gate of heaven" (28:17b NIV). Then Jacob memorialized the location by setting up his stone pillow as a pillar and renamed the town from Luz to Bethel. What's more, Jacob made a vow to tithe a tenth of his future wealth to God. If this had been merely a "fairy story for people afraid of the dark," as Hawking suggests, it's doubtful that Jacob would have gone to such lengths to commemorate it.

Dr. Mary Neal, like Jacob, would adamantly disagree with Hawking's statement that "there is no Heaven or afterlife"—although there was a time when her view was akin to Hawking's perspective. A spinal surgeon by trade, Mary defined herself as a "scientist by training, a skeptic by nature, and a very concrete, rational thinker."[30] By her own admission, although she was a professing

Christian, faith wasn't integrated into her life beyond Sunday church attendance and prayers at mealtime.

The events of January 14, 1999, changed her life.

Mary and her husband, both experienced kayakers, went kayaking down the whitewater rapids of the Fuy, a remote river in southern Chile. The Fuy has a number of steep drops, plummeting 10 to 20 feet. After cresting the main drop, danger struck. Mary and her kayak became submerged under the hungry, swirling currents at the bottom. The front end of her boat became pinned by a rock. With the crushing force of water pouring on top of her, she was unable to free herself from the kayak.

Rescue attempts by her boating companions proved futile.

Trapped, Mary called out to God—not demanding to be rescued but for His will to be done. Buried beneath the water for more than 15 minutes, Mary drowned. She clearly felt her spirit leave her body. That was when Mary—the former skeptic—found herself welcomed by a crowd of spiritual beings where she immediately felt comforted and at peace. She says, "I was home. It was my absolute true home."[31] She describes "sitting in a beautiful, sun-drenched field with an angel. The brilliance and intensity of the surrounding beauty and the purity of the angel's radiant love were simultaneously overwhelming and rejuvenating. We spoke for what seemed like many hours, and I never wanted to leave."[32]

Incidentally, that feeling of never wanting to leave the contentment and unmatched beauty of Heaven is almost universally expressed by those who have had a NDE. Dr. Raymond Moody is a medical doctor and author of *Life After Life*, the seminal book on near-death experiences. Having researched more than a thousand cases of people who had NDEs and who were clinically dead, a number of whom have reported interacting with angels, he notes that there are numerous

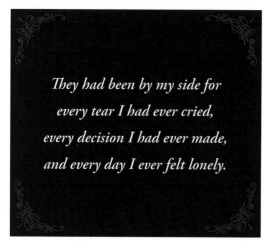

They had been by my side for every tear I had ever cried, every decision I had ever made, and every day I ever felt lonely.

survivors who "are frequently very angry at their doctors for bringing them back."

Dr. Moody tells this fascinating story of a physician by the name of "Carl" who had resuscitated a cardiac arrest patient: "When the stricken man revived, he said angrily: 'Carl, don't you ever do that to me again.'" Why? The patient told Carl, "I was mad because you brought me back to death instead of life."[33]

Which brings us to Crystal McVea. Crystal wore several hats: wife, school teacher, and mother of four. In 2009, sharp abdominal pains caused her to rush to the hospital to be treated for pancreatitis. Her doctors prescribed a powerful pain medication that caused an unexpected reaction. Crystal's body began to twitch, became cold, and started shutting down. Her lips and face turned blue and then her breathing stopped. The medical personnel called a "Code Blue," and a team of nurses and doctors worked frantically to save her.

For nine minutes, Crystal was dead to this world.

In her book, *Waking Up in Heaven*, Crystal reports that she left this world and was instantly in the presence of two angels: "There was so much brightness coming off them that I couldn't make out any features. But they weren't shapeless blobs; they definitely had a form, which was roughly that of a human body: long and slender . . . And what I instantly felt for them was love." Why was she so overwhelmed when she met these angels? She writes, it was as if "they had been by my side for every tear I had ever cried, every decision I had ever made, every day I ever felt lonely. I felt so unbelievably safe and free in their presence, so happy and fulfilled. I understood why they were there—to greet me upon my arrival and guide me back home. They were the best welcoming committee you could ask for."[34]

But what knocked her to her knees was, like Jacob, being in the presence of God. She describes crumpling and falling before Him, raising her hands while bowing in praise and worship, adding, "Me! Crystal! The sinner and the skeptic; the one with all the questions!"[35] Personally, I'm glad to see that she worshiped God rather than the angel, which John the Apostle confessed he found irresistible during his Revelation of Heaven. He writes:

"I, John, am the one who heard and saw all these things. And when I heard and saw them, I fell down to worship at the feet of the angel who showed them to me. But he said, 'No, don't worship me. I am a servant of God, just like you and your brothers the prophets, as well as all who obey what is written in this book. Worship only God!'" (Revelation 22:8–9 NLT).

Do you wonder if God is present in your world? Do you question whether or not His angels still watch over you? Do you wonder if He will keep His promise to never leave or forsake you? In spite of what you—or others like Stephen Hawking—may feel, angels are alive and real, and they're presently at work on earth. Although Heaven is their home, the author of Hebrews says angels are "Ministering spirits, sent forth to minister for them who shall be heirs of salvation" (1:13–14 NIV).

Isn't that encouraging to know that God so loves you that He commands His angels to minister to all who put their faith in Him. The psalmist put this joyous news this way: "The angel of the Lord encamps around those who fear him, and he delivers them" (Psalm 34:7 NIV). No, we're not to worship them—that praise is reserved for Jesus. But by all means we can give thanks for the role they play this side of Heaven.

"I, with shriveled, bent fingers, atrophied muscles, gnarled knees, and no feeling from the shoulders down, will one day have a new body— light, bright and clothed in righteousness— powerful and dazzling."

—

Joni Eareckson Tada[36]

"He who was seated on the throne said, 'I am making everything new!' Then he said, 'Write this down, for these words are trustworthy and true.'"

—

Revelation 21:5 (NIV)

Chapter 7

HEAVEN IS A PLACE OF PERFECTION

*I*n 1970, my mom thought taking my brother and me to the Philadelphia Art Museum would be a good idea. I was 13. Steve was 11. She explained this exhibit was a collection of priceless masterpieces by some famous post-Impressionist artist I'd never heard of before—Vincent van Gogh. I confess we weren't crazy about this trip. At that age, my brother and I were more interested in playing baseball than speaking in hushed tones while staring at a bunch of paintings hanging on a wall.

We climbed the museum's steps, passed through the eight majestic Corinthian columns that stood as tall as California Redwoods, and entered the galleria. Since Van Gogh was a legendary artist, I thought for sure his art would be displayed behind thick security glass. I figured wrong. In fact, his original paintings were mounted on the wall with nothing but a metal foot rail placed 12 inches off of the ground, positioned about three feet parallel to the wall. I thought anyone could easily reach out and touch them—or worse. While there were guards sitting on stools about every 40 feet, someone with ill intent could do some serious damage to these irreplaceable paintings long before they could prevent it.

That's when my brother did the unthinkable.

Steve reached out and touched *The Starry Night*, one of the most beloved Van Gogh's. Worse, I saw a blue-green fleck of paint float to the ground. I thought for sure we'd be arrested and sent to jail. Thankfully, the guard's head was turned the other way and only saw Steve's hand hovering near the surface of the canvas. Warned to keep our distance, we moved on. And yet I couldn't shake the fact that this masterpiece had been so easily damaged.

That encounter with Van Gogh's pièce de résistance got me thinking. This side of Heaven, even the most perfect creation—such as a Van Gogh—suffers from the corrupting effects of the fall. Perfectly paved roads develop potholes. Perfectly manicured gardens sprout weeds. Perfectly manufactured automobiles develop rust. And, our perfectly created bodies suffer from deteriorating joints, failing memories, and internal organs that cease to function properly. None of us are exempt from decay.

Regarding our human frailty, the Apostle Paul writes, "The bodies we have now embarrass us, for they become sick and die; but they will be full of glory when we come back to life again. Yes, they are weak, dying bodies now, but when we live again they will be full of strength. They are just human bodies at death, but when they come back to life they will be superhuman bodies" (1 Corinthians 15:43–44a TLB). Yes, this side of Heaven we will never experience the enduring perfection we were originally created to enjoy. That's the bad news.

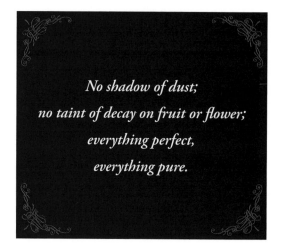

No shadow of dust;
no taint of decay on fruit or flower;
everything perfect,
everything pure.

The good news is that Heaven is a place of perfection.

In 1898, Rebecca Springer had a glimpse of Heaven's perfection. Rebecca's vision came not while resting her head upon a rock, as was the case with Jacob when his vision of the stairs spanning between Heaven and earth appeared. Rather, malnourished and struggling to survive a debilitating illness, she experienced her vision "during the days when life hung in the balance between Time and Eternity, with the scales dipping decidedly toward the Eternity side."[37] She writes about her experience in a classic book entitled, *Intra Muros*—which means "within the gates." Here's how she describes her first view of Heaven:

"I was sitting in a sheltered nook, made by flowering shrubs, upon the softest and most beautiful turf of grass, thickly studded with fragrant flowers, many of them flowers I had known and loved on earth. I remember noticing heliotrope, violets, lilies of the valley, and mignonette, with many others of like nature wholly unfamiliar to me. But even in that first moment I observed how perfect in its way was every plant and flower. For instance, the heliotrope, which with us often runs into long, ragged sprays, there grew upon short, smooth stems, and each leaf was perfect and smooth and glossy, instead of being rough and coarse-looking; and the flowers peeped up from the deep grass, so like velvet, with sweet, happy faces as though inviting the admiration one could not withhold."

Such perfection is good news to anyone who has ever attempted to plant a garden or maintain their yard against an army of crabgrass and legions of plant-eating creepy-crawlers. But the perfection she saw in Heaven extended beyond plants to all aspects of creation:

"Look where I would, I saw, half hidden by the trees, elegant and beautiful houses of strangely attractive architecture that I felt must be the homes of the happy inhabitants of this enchanted place. I caught glimpses of sparkling fountains in many directions, and close to my retreat flowed a river with placid breast and water clear as crystal. The walks that ran in many directions through the grounds appeared to me to be, and I afterward found were, of pearl, spotless and pure, bordered on either side by narrow streams of pellucid water running over stones of gold."

God has promised all who believe in Him a new Heaven and new earth (Isaiah 66:22) where we'll never experience the devastating effects of sin, death, or corruption. Rebecca writes:

"The one thought that fastened itself upon me as I looked, breathless and speechless, upon this scene was 'Purity, purity!' No shadow of dust; no taint of decay on fruit or flower; everything perfect, everything pure. The grass and flowers looked as though fresh-washed by summer showers, and not a single blade was any color but the brightest green. The air was soft and balmy, though invigorating; and instead of sunlight there was a golden and rosy glory everywhere, something like the afterglow of a Southern sunset in midsummer."[38]

In fact, Rebecca was so overwhelmed by this glorious perfection, she writes, ". . . such an overpowering sense of God's goodness and my own unworthiness swept over me that I dropped my face into my hands, and burst into uncontrollable and very human weeping."[39]

Are you excited about the prospect of the day when we'll be able to throw away our crutches and walkers? Where we'll never again say, "Oh, my aching back!" Billy Graham observes, "In our resurrection bodies, we will know nothing of physical weakness. Limitations imposed on us on this earth are not known in Heaven. We will have a habitation from God that is incorruptible, immortal, and powerful."[40]

I don't know about you, but to me it's incredible to picture a place of such wondrous perfection, one where weed killer will be a thing of the past. There will be no need for repair trucks, tow trucks, or police. Gone will be all crime, decay, and brokenness. As the Apostle Peter writes, "In keeping with his promise we are looking forward to a new heaven and a new earth, where righteousness dwells. So then, dear friends, since you are looking forward to this, make every effort to be found spotless, blameless and at peace with him" (2 Peter 3:13–14 NIV).

I can't wait for that day. How about you?

"I believe with all my heart that God will raise the little ones as such, and that the mother's arms that have ached for them will have the opportunity of holding them. The father's hand that never held the little hand will be given that privilege."

—

J. Vernon McGee[41]

"From the lips of children and infants you have ordained praise.'"

—

Matthew 21:16b (NIV)

Chapter 8

HEAVEN IS A PLACE WHERE OUR UNBORN CHILDREN AWAIT US

*O*ur precious four-month-old angel Danny was sleeping in his crib while another angel of the plastic variety sat atop the Christmas tree. White lights and shiny ornaments took their assigned places on the branches, while a modest army of colorfully wrapped presents awaited below. My wife Leticia, fourteen weeks pregnant with our fifth child, was resting as I tiptoed out of the house with the other youngsters for a Christmas morning service at church. As a father, my heart was full. Solomon was right, "Children are a gift from the Lord" (Psalm 127:3a NLT). But for reasons known only to Him, the Lord saw fit to call our unborn gift home.

When I returned after the service, my wife met me with tears—she had miscarried the baby. That heartache would repeat itself the following Thanksgiving when we lost another unborn child after thirteen weeks. Any parent who has lost a baby carries within them a grief that runs deeper than the ocean. It's human nature to wonder: *What went wrong? What could we have done differently?* I know my wife worked hard to eat the right foods and get the necessary prenatal vitamins, exercise, and rest to ensure a healthy pregnancy. In spite of her efforts, after giving birth to four healthy children, there are two empty seats at our table.

For millions of others who, like us, have lost a baby there's the eternal question: *Will we see our unborn children in Heaven?* Two perspectives brought me comfort—an observation by author Randy Alcorn and a rather remarkable exchange between Colton Burpo and his parents. More on that in a moment. In his bestseller *Heaven*, Randy notes: "On the New Earth many opportunities lost in this life will be wonderfully restored. Although it's not directly stated and I am therefore speculating, it's possible that parents whose hearts were broken through the death of their children will not only be reunited with them but will also experience the joy of seeing them grow up . . . in a perfect world."[42] Is that a stretch? I don't think so. Why not?

Genesis records a conversation between Lot and God regarding the pending destruction of Lot's hometown, the city of Sodom. Lot, who had hoped to stave off God's judgment, appealed to the righteousness of God, asking, "Will not the Judge of all the earth do right?" (Genesis 18:24 NIV). If we know anything about God, the Bible makes it clear He *is* righteous and just, and His love knows no bounds. After all, God sent His only son Jesus to make a way possible for us to be with Him in Heaven.

This is why I have complete confidence that God will deal justly with the unborn who never had the opportunity to invite Jesus into their hearts. On this point, Randy adds, "Although children are sinners who need to be saved, God may well have a just way to cover them with Christ's blood so they go to Heaven when they die."[43]

Which brings us to the remarkable conversation Todd Burpo records in his bestseller, *Heaven Is for Real*. Todd and his wife Sonja's son Colton had an emergency appendectomy. During the surgery, Colton, who was not quite four years old, experienced a vision of Heaven. The details of Colton's vision—including encounters with relatives who he never met in life, angels, and the description of events that occurred prior to his birth—were difficult for his parents to dismiss out-of-hand. During the next few months and years, Colton repeatedly stunned Todd and Sonja with details about Heaven that aligned with what Scripture teaches. Keep in mind, Colton was too young to have read the Bible on his own and would have no way to know such information apart from a first-hand encounter with the Divine.

One October evening, Todd, who pastored a church, was engaged in his sermon prep at the kitchen table while Sonja was paying bills in the living room. Four-year-old Colton approached his mother and, out of the blue, announced that he had two sisters. This didn't make sense to his parents because they only had one daughter, Cassie. When Sonja suggested Colton must be referring to his older sister Cassie and her cousin, Colton wouldn't relent. He said, "I have two *sisters*. You had a baby die in your tummy, didn't you?"

You can imagine what a shock this innocent comment was to his parents who never told Colton about their miscarriage. How could he possibly know about that bit of family history? Sonja asked, "Who told you I had a baby die in my tummy?" Without skipping a beat, little Colton said, "She did, Mommy. She said she died in your tummy." In the moments that followed, Colton, sensing his parents' angst, attempted to allay their concerns, saying, "She's okay. God adopted her." When asked what her name was, Colton said, "She doesn't have a name. You guys didn't name her."

Once again, his parents were dumbfounded that he'd know this detail. As it turns out, they hadn't named their unborn baby because they didn't know whether they were having a boy or a girl. Almost as an afterthought, Colton added, "Yeah, she said she just can't wait for you and Daddy to get to Heaven."[44] You can imagine how his parents took great comfort at this news.

I'm sure there are those who would be quick to dismiss Colton's vision of Heaven. If you are one of them, let me point you to the words of the Apostle Peter: "In the last days, God says, I will pour out my Spirit on all people. Your sons and daughters will prophesy, your young men will see visions, your old men will dream dreams" (Acts 2:17 NIV). I can't say with certainty that Colton saw Heaven. But it's entirely possible that God has chosen young Colton's vision to bring those of us grieving the loss of a child hope. In fact, the idea that one day we will be reunited with our unborn is consistent with what King

David said upon the loss of his infant child. David, who had fasted and prayed for the life of his seven-day-old baby, said, "Can I bring him back again? I will go to him, but he will not return to me" (2 Samuel 12:22b NIV).

Have you suffered the emotionally numbing loss of a child? Does grief shadow your waking hours? Does your heart long to hold your little one in your arms? Do you wonder if one day you'll see him or her in Heaven? Beloved pastor and author Charles Spurgeon pondered those questions and concluded: "I could not believe it of Jesus, that he would say to little children, 'Depart, ye accursed, into everlasting fire in hell!' I cannot conceive it possible of him as the loving and tender one, that when he shall sit to judge all nations, he should put the little ones on the left hand, and should banish them for ever from his presence."[45]

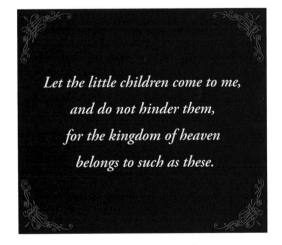

Let the little children come to me,
and do not hinder them,
for the kingdom of heaven
belongs to such as these.

When sadness over the death of a child threatens to rob your joy, just remember it was Jesus who said, "Let the little children come to me, and do not hinder them, for the kingdom of heaven belongs to such as these" (Matthew 19:14 NIV). What's more, the Bible records a scene where "People were also bringing babies to Jesus for him to place his hands on them" (Luke 18:15a NIV). Indeed, throughout His life on earth, babies and children held a special place in His heart.

How could Heaven be any different?

"Our belief that Heaven will be boring betrays a heresy—that God is boring. There's no greater nonsense. Our desire for pleasure and the experience of joy come directly from God's hand . . . The real question is this: How could God not be bored with us?"

—

Randy Alcorn[46]

"In Your presence is abundant joy; in Your right hand are eternal pleasures."

—

David, Psalm 16:11b (HCSB)

Chapter 9

HEAVEN IS A PLACE WHERE BOREDOM IS BANISHED

*F*or a number of years, the Seattle-based Starbucks company printed pithy quotes on the sides of their paper coffee cups. Famously known as "The Way I See It" messages, these inspirational ditties were designed to "help us reflect on what's important in life, inspire us to be better people and sometimes, simply make us laugh."[47] Hundreds of tidbits were a hit with customers thirsty for both a good brew and equally tasty conversation starters.

In 2007, one controversial quote, penned by *Los Angeles Times* columnist Joel Stein, got Starbucks in hot water: "Heaven is totally overrated. It seems boring. Clouds, listening to people play harps. It should be somewhere you can't wait to go, like a luxury hotel. Maybe blue skies and soft music were enough to keep people in line in the 17th century, but Heaven has to step it up a bit. They basically are getting by because they only have to be better than hell." As you can imagine, calls for a boycott ensued.

Setting aside the merits of boycotting Starbucks, Stein's view that Heaven is a dull, uninteresting destination is evidently shared by the *Far Side*'s Gary

Larson. The popular cartoonist once sketched a bored, bespectacled man out-fitted with halo and angel wings, stranded on a lone cloud in Heaven, pouting: "Wish I'd brought a magazine." Ted Turner, founder of CNN, during a speech before the National Press Club summed up his view, saying, "Heaven is perfect. Who wants to go to a place that's perfect? Boring. Boring."[48]

Likewise Isaac Asimov, the brilliant and prolific Russian-born American author of more than 500 books, who was like-minded in his contempt of Heaven. He said, "I don't believe in an afterlife, so I don't have to spend my whole life fearing hell, or fearing Heaven even more. For whatever the tortures of hell, I think the boredom of Heaven would be even worse."[49]

This lackluster picture of Heaven isn't limited to unbelievers. My friend and bestselling author of *Wild at Heart*, John Eldredge, said, "Nearly every Christian I have spoken with has some idea that eternity is an unending church service. . . . We have settled on an image of the never-ending sing-along in the sky, one great hymn after another, forever and ever, amen. And our heart sinks. *Forever and ever? That's it? That's the good news?* And then we sigh and feel guilty that we are not more 'spiritual.' We lose heart, and we turn once more to the present to find what life we can."[50]

Why does Heaven have such a bad rap?

Admittedly, the Church hasn't done a very good job celebrating what the new heaven and new earth will be like. And, candidly, as a parent, I admit I haven't done all that I could do to help my children anticipate their glorious inheritance. But let's not miss one of the most insidious and effective lies Satan uses to deceive us, namely, *that God Himself is boring.* The Bible even warns us about his deception, describing the devil as a dragon who "opened its mouth to blaspheme God, and to slander his name *and his dwelling place* and those who live in heaven" (Revelation 13:6 NIV, emphasis added).

Why does Satan slander God's dwelling place in Heaven?

What's his agenda? What does he gain by doing that?

Clearly the goal of the great deceiver is to neutralize our passion and longing to spend eternity with Jesus. Satan—who was booted out of Heaven, forever forbidden from reentry—doesn't want you and me to enjoy what he can no longer have. And, the last thing he wants is for God's children to be so excited about Heaven that we share His truth with as many as we can this side of eternity. We shouldn't be surprised by his deception that Heaven is a bore. Jesus didn't mince words about Satan's character, saying, "for there is no truth in him. When he lies, he speaks his native language, for he is a liar and the father of lies" (John 8:44b NIV). This is where a few glimpses of Heaven by those who have seen it can be beneficial to dispel this falsehood.

Don Piper who, as you recall, spent 90 minutes in Heaven, says, "Heaven's light and texture defy . . . explanation. Warm, radiant light engulfed me. As I looked around, I could hardly grasp the vivid, dazzling colors. Every hue and tone surpassed anything I had ever seen. With all the heightened awareness of my senses, I felt as if

Are we so arrogant as to imagine that human beings came up with the idea of having fun?

I had never seen, heard, or felt anything so real before. . . . Never, even in my happiest moments, had I ever felt so fully alive."[51] If you're a painter, an artist, an interior designer, or a chef who's presentation of food includes the interplay of color on the dish, how could you be bored with a whole new palate and array of colors to work with?

For his part, Dr. Eben Alexander says of Heaven, "The place I went was real. Real in a way that makes the life we're living here and now completely dreamlike by comparison."[52] What's more, every time he had a question "the answer came instantly in an explosion of light, color, love, and beauty that blew through me like a crashing wave."[53] How could being slammed with such a tidal wave of unspeakable beauty ever be called boring?

In his book, *Evidence of the Afterlife*, Dr. Jeffrey Long, a "man of science" who used to believe that "death is the cessation of our existence," changed his view after studying more than 1,000 accounts of near-death experiences.[54] He records this description from a patient who said, "The colors on the other side are the brightest colors; our most fluorescent colors on this earth are muddy [compared] to the brightness and vividness of the colors that are in Heaven."[55] To be redundant, that sounds captivating, not boring.

Another individual, Arthur Yensen, who had a glimpse of Heaven, said, "To the left was a shimmering lake containing a different kind of water—clear, golden, radiant, and alluring. It seemed to be alive. The whole landscape was carpeted with grass so vivid, clear, and green, that it defies description."[56] Water that's "alive" and a landscape that "defies description" sounds breathtaking to me.

Regarding the notion that Heaven is boring, Randy Alcorn said it best: "[God] made our taste buds, adrenaline, sex drives, and the nerve endings that convey pleasure to our brains. Likewise, our imaginations and our capacity for joy and exhilaration were made by the very God we accuse of being boring. Are we so arrogant as to imagine that human beings came up with the idea of having fun? . . . we've got it backward. It's not God who's boring; it's us. Did we invent wit, humor, and laughter? No. God did. We'll never begin to exhaust God's sense of humor and his love for adventure."[57]

How about you? When you think of Heaven, what picture comes to mind?

Do you view Heaven as a prolonged church service—one where even after you've carefully filled in the space on all of the vowels and consonants in the bulletin, there's not a chance that the pastor will be finished in time for lunch? Do you think we'll just be strumming "When the Roll Is Called Up Yonder" on our harps with the monotone drone of the Muzak channel piped into an elevator? If you're painfully honest, do you fear that you might just be B-O-R-E-D in Heaven because there'll be nothing interesting to do?

If so, consider asking yourself: *Could this be because my relationship with God is boring? Has my Christian life become as mundane as doing the laundry, as routine as loading the dishwasher, as dull as the worn finish on my car? If so, who's fault is that? When was the last time I opened myself up to an adventurous, risk-taking faith, one where Jesus and I marched boldly into some new kingdom endeavor?*

Indeed, the truth about Heaven is that "No eye has seen, no ear has heard, and no mind has imagined what God has prepared for those who love Him"

(1 Corinthians 2:9 NLT). In other words, Heaven defies the capacity of our feeble imaginations to fully appreciate what awaits us. Just look at some of the reactions of those in the Bible who encountered God. When Isaiah saw the Lord he cried out, "Woe to me! I am ruined" (Isaiah 6:5a NIV). When Peter, James, and John saw Jesus transfigured before their eyes, they "fell facedown to the ground, terrified" (Matthew 17:6 NIV). When John saw Heaven, he fell down to worship (Revelation 22:8).

The Bible is clear: nobody comes into the presence of the living God and yawns.

"My deepest awareness of myself
is that I am deeply loved by Jesus Christ
and I have done nothing to earn it or deserve it."

—

Brennan Manning[58]

" Who shall separate us from the love of
Christ? . . . Neither death nor life, neither angels
nor demons, neither the present nor the future,
nor any powers, neither height nor depth,
nor anything else in all creation, will be able
to separate us from the love of God
that is in Christ Jesus our Lord."

—

Paul, Romans 8:35, 38–39 (NIV)

Chapter 10

HEAVEN IS A PLACE OF UNCONDITIONAL LOVE

A number of years ago, renowned pollster George Gallup, Jr. turned "the full resources of the Gallup Poll toward an exploration of the afterlife."[59] He commissioned a study identifying the number of Americans who have had a near-death experience. Gallop concluded the number to be 5 percent of the U.S. population—that's 15 million adults as of this printing. In preparation for this book, I read the accounts of more than 60 people who had died and come back to life. Some were dead for just a handful of minutes. In a number of cases, medical personnel had begun preparations for the morgue because the patient had been dead for hours—and in one case for three days. You can imagine the fright the caregivers experienced when a previously dead body sprung back to life.

You can't read that many stories without identifying certain unifying patterns. A majority passed through a tunnel of light before arriving in Heaven. Some traveled through what the Bible describes as the valley of the shadow of death (Psalm 23:4). Of particular interest to me was how time and time again, those who had near-death experiences zeroed in on the power and depth of the love of Jesus they encountered—and were frustrated by the utter feebleness of the human vocabulary to describe His love. They said things such as "His love enveloped me, a love so pure I cannot describe it," "Love seemed to pour out of Him," and "I didn't ever want to leave the unconditional love I felt in His presence."

Take, for example, Jim Sepulveda, a 35-year-old businessman. Jim had an enlarged heart requiring double bypass surgery. During his operation, Jim flat-lined. After working feverishly to resuscitate him for eight minutes, his doctors declared him dead. After pulling the sheet over Jim's head, his primary surgeon began to fill out the necessary paperwork recording his death. Meanwhile, Jim found himself "standing in a field, surrounded by acres of green grass. Every blade glowed as if backlit by a tiny spotlight. To my right stretched a dazzling expanse of vibrant flowers, with colors I had never seen before. Above me the endless sky was a deep and pure blue. *The air around me was permeated with love*"[60] (emphasis added).

The fact that Jim felt Heaven's air around him saturated with love shouldn't come as a surprise because the central message of the Bible is that "God is love" (1 John 4:8b NIV) and it's available to us unconditionally. God says, "I have loved you with an everlasting love; I have drawn you with loving kindness" (Jeremiah 31:3 NIV). Let's not rush past the Good News that He loves us and "He chose us in him before the creation of the world" (Ephesians 1:4a NIV). Why is this important to grasp?

Few things in life are unconditional. For example, if you're like me, one

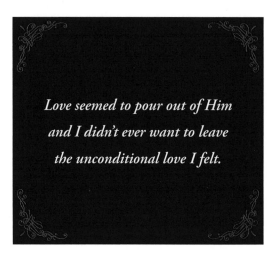

Love seemed to pour out of Him and I didn't ever want to leave the unconditional love I felt.

of the few pieces of snail mail filling my mailbox these days are mortgage refinancing pitches promising "no closing costs or hidden fees" and credit card offers featuring "balance transfers with zero-percent interest." Sound familiar? If I'm bored or just procrastinating on a writing deadline, I'll scan through the hype in search of the "fine print"—those pesky "terms and conditions" that must be met to qualify. Buried deep in legal language requiring a team of accountants to decipher, even if I do meet the requirements, the conditions of the deal can change in an instant for any number of reasons—at which point I'd suffer enormous and unwanted penalties.

Not so with God's love. His unconditional love knows no bounds. It's not a limited time offer that expires if we mess up. No wonder those who have tasted His love cannot get enough of it and struggle to describe it. Which brings us back to Jim's encounter with the Divine. He continues:

"I squinted down toward the ground, and then saw a pair of sandals beginning to appear at the bottom edge of the light. As my eyes moved upward, I glimpsed the hem of a seamless white gown. Higher, I could make out the form of a Man's body. Around His head shone an even brighter brilliance, obscuring a direct view of His face.

Even though I could not see clearly, because of the dazzling splendor, I knew immediately the identity of this Man. I was standing in the presence of Jesus Christ. '*Jim, I love you.*' His voice washed over me, indescribably gentle, tender and peaceful. . . . Then the brilliance surrounding Him reached out and engulfed me, immersing me in a total sense of love and peace."[61]

The "total sense of love" Jim enjoyed is what Petti Wagner reports experiencing during her visit to Heaven. In her book, *Murdered Heiress*, Petti, a successful multi-millionaire who says she had been kidnapped, held as a prisoner, and then killed by electrocution, struggled to put into human terms the depth of the love she felt. She described the feeling this way: "[Being in] God's garden was the most exciting and inviting existence I could ever want. There was such perfect peace, such goodness, such wisdom . . . a place of eternal, pure love. . . . Every second I was with Him it seemed that a million intravenous tubes of pure love went into my body."[62] And, then there's the observation by neurosurgeon Dr. Eben Alexander during his near-death experience; said, "I was a citizen of a universe staggering in its vastness and complexity and ruled entirely by love."[63]

How should this news about God's vast, unconditional love—which knows no bounds—impact our life here and now? One of Jesus' best friends on earth, John the Beloved, who as you recall experienced the Divine in Heaven, answers this question, saying, "Dear friends, since God so loved us, we also ought to love one another. . . . We love because he first loved us. . . . Anyone who loves God must also love their brother and sister" (1 John 4:11, 19, 21b NIV). You might be thinking, "Yeah, but you don't know my brother" or "My spouse is unlovable" or "My friend has betrayed me, so does God really expect me to love them?" Yes. John goes so far as to explain that we're to love them as Jesus would love them because "In this world we are like Jesus" (v. 18).

We love unconditionally because we are loved unconditionally.

No fine print. No exemption clauses.

Can that be messy? Absolutely. There are times when we'll blow our attempts to love others well. That's when God's grace covers our imperfect efforts. Bestselling author Brennan Manning, whose *Ragamuffin Gospel* is perhaps one of the most candid treatments regarding our need for God's loving grace, put it this way: "We should be astonished at the goodness of God, stunned that He should bother to call us by name, our mouths wide open at His love, bewildered that at this very moment we are standing on holy ground."[64]

Astonished. Stunned. Bewildered.

Yes, that should be our posture as we seek to love those within our sphere of influence, and as we anticipate living forever with Jesus in Heaven. John Newton said it best when he reflected, "If I ever reach Heaven I expect to find three wonders there: first, to meet some I had not thought to see there; second, to miss some I had expected to see there; and third, the greatest wonder of all, to find myself there."[65]

Considering how infrequently the taste of true unconditional love passes our lips, why not drink deeply from the words of Psalm 103 today? Pay special attention to all of the ways God's love for us is described—especially verse 17 which says, "from everlasting to everlasting the Lord's love is with those who fear him." And don't get in the way of allowing God's love to flow through you to those who need it most.

"Behold here the reward of every Christian conqueror!
Christ's throne, crown scepter, palace, treasure,
robes, heritage, are yours."

—

C. H. Spurgeon[66]

"To him who is victorious, I will give the right
to sit with me on my throne, just as I was victorious
and sat down with my Father on his throne."

—

Jesus, Revelation 3:21 (NIV)

Chapter 11

HEAVEN IS A PLACE WHERE WE WILL REIGN WITH JESUS

God has created a permanent home for you and me in Heaven, a place of unimaginable glory, a place already inhabited by many of your loved ones and countless other heavenly hosts. Millions of people have seen Heaven, dwelled there for a brief time, and returned to earth to tell us about their experiences. These "near-death experiencers" report that Heaven is a wonderful place, a place of infinite joy, incomparable beauty, unmatched music and worship, and everlasting love.

Heaven is our true home.

But there's one additional aspect of Heaven that is sure to blow your mind: Jesus, our Creator and Savior, *plans to share His thrown with us.* You might want to read that again. The King of kings and Lord of lords desires to share what is rightly and solely His with you and with me. This news should render us speechless. Why is He planning to do that for us? He certainly isn't obligated to do so. And yet the Good Shepherd, out of His amazing love for us, shares His throne with you and me.

For all of eternity. For His good pleasure.

Don't take my word for this astounding truth. Let me take you back to the original paradise, to the Garden of Eden. In Genesis, we learn that God created everything seen and unseen—including inhabitable planets numbering as many as 100 billion[67] alongside of our little planet with its abundant plant life, countless sea creatures, and diverse menagerie of animals. And then He made His pièce de résistance by fashioning us in His image. But He wasn't finished.

At this point in the story, He does a remarkable thing: Our awesome Creator chooses to share His authority with Adam and Eve by putting them in charge of *all* created things. Watch as God pulls back the curtain to give us a glimpse of the conversation that took place within the Trinity: "Let us make mankind in our image, in our likeness, *so that they may rule* over the fish of the sea and the birds in the sky, over the livestock and all the wild animals, and over all the creatures that move along the ground" (Genesis 1:26 NIV, emphasis added). Other translations render the word "rule" as "have dominion" (KJV) or "reign" (NLT).

At the risk of getting stuck in the weeds, the Latin root word for "reign" means a number of things, most notably authority, kingdom, realm, and to rule. By definition, kings and queens reign supreme. Their royal office allows them to have dominion over everything in the land. Their word is final. That is precisely the power and position that God deputized Adam and Eve with in the beginning. In that respect, they were not spectators—they were in charge.

Further evidence of this astonishing news can be found in the book of Daniel. Daniel, who had a vision of Heaven, foresaw the day when "the sovereignty, power and greatness of the kingdoms under the whole heaven will be handed over to the saints, the people of the Most High" (7:27 ESV). Jesus put it this way, "Fear not, little flock, for it is your Father's *good pleasure* to *give you the*

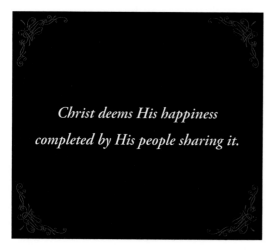

Christ deems His happiness completed by His people sharing it.

kingdom" (Luke 12:32 ESV, emphasis added). As if that's not clear enough, Jesus assures us of this breathtaking reality, saying, "I assign to you, as my Father assigned to me, a kingdom, that you may eat and drink at my table in my kingdom and sit on thrones judging the twelve tribes of Israel" (Luke 22:29–30 ESV).

C. H. Spurgeon described this startling and supreme act of benevolence this way, saying, "The golden streets of paradise, the pearly gates, the river of life, the transcendent bliss, and the unutterable glory, are, by our blessed Lord, made over to us for our everlasting possession. All that he has he shares with his people . . . Christ deems his happiness completed by his people sharing it."[68]

What an awesome thing to truly comprehend.

I admit I struggle to wrap my head around the promise that Jesus is planning to have me sit by His side. About the only way I can begin to understand this ultimate gift of love is to look at my role as a father relating to my own children. For instance, as the old saying goes, "A man's home is his castle." And in my little fiefdom, I could easily do everything with no help from anyone.

I could insist that my kids watch me as I cook, landscape the yard, paint the bedrooms, and maybe build an addition onto the house. But where would be the joy in that? I'd be turning my children into mere spectators. By contrast, some of my greatest joy in life comes from giving my children the tools, the resources, and the general direction for a project and then cutting them loose to express themselves creatively.

The fun comes in the participation.

I believe the same is true of our Heavenly Father. Because He delights in us, He invites us to *participate* in His inheritance. What's more, God has revealed His future plans to us because He wants us to have a joyful anticipation of this magnificent world to come. But, as author Randy Alcorn points out, believers overlook this staggering news: "When we consider that mankind's reign on earth is introduced in the first chapters of the Bible, mentioned throughout the Old Testament, discussed by Jesus in the Gospels, by Paul in the Epistles, and repeated by John in the Bible's final chapters, it is remarkable that we would fail to see it."[69] Alcorn's comment got me thinking about the reaction in

Heaven to this, our supreme negligence.

Remember the 10,000 x 10,000 angels singing praises around God's holy throne and the guardian angels assigned to you and me? What might they be thinking about the fact that far too many Christians aren't even aware of their Savior's plan to share the throne? These angels, who have been serving in the presence of God for thousands of years, must be wondering: "Why don't these humans get it? How can they be so clueless after the Father has placed His fingerprints all over Creation? How did they miss His divine signature? After all, it's stamped onto every cell and atom throughout the galaxy! Why does the Holy One insist on giving the keys to the Kingdom to those mortals who are petty, rude, belligerent, self-righteous, arrogant, and filled with pride? What do they know about running a Kingdom? What preparations have they made so that their hearts are aligned with the heart of Jesus? What do they really know about justice, mercy, kindness, wisdom, grace, and longsuffering?"

I stand convicted. Days go by when I forget about the "great love the Father has lavished on us" (1 John 3:3 NIV). I find myself wondering why I'm so slow to live out the admonishment that "This is how we know what love is: Jesus Christ laid down his life for us. And we ought to lay down our lives for our brothers and sisters" (3:16). And, in spite of my error, I'm forgiven (1 John 1:9). Which brings me to a final observation. The fact that you and I will reign with Jesus is beyond our wildest dreams. At the same time, let's not lose sight of the fact that the main attraction of Heaven isn't *reigning* with Jesus—it's *being* in the presence of Jesus.

Nothing else matters.

So, when the miles get long and your heart grows faint, no matter what hurdles life throws at you, just remember this world isn't your final destination. You were designed by God for so much more. As singer Gloria Gather has said, "One of these days our Father will scoop us up in His strong arms and we will hear Him say those sweet and comforting words, 'Come on, child. We're going home.'"[70]

"The wizard [of Oz] says look inside yourself and find self. God says look inside yourself and find [the Holy Spirit]. The first will get you to Kansas. The latter will get you to Heaven. Take your pick."

—

Max Lucado[71]

"Behold! I stand at the door and knock. If anyone hears My voice and opens the door, I will come in to him and dine with him, and he with Me."

—

Jesus, Revelation 3:20 (NKJV)

Chapter 12

HEAVEN IS
AN INVITATION

*D*uring the sixties and seventies, English actor Peter Sellers amassed worldwide acclaim for his role as the bumbling Chief Inspector Jacques Clouseau in *The Pink Panther*. Millions of fans enjoyed the comedic antics of Peter Sellers on the screen. Behind the scenes he was a troubled man, one who struggled with bouts of depression when he wasn't working on a film.

In 1964, Sellers suffered a heart attack and was reportedly clinically dead. As his doctor worked frantically to restart his heart, Peter says, "I felt myself leave my body. I just floated out of my physical form and I saw them cart my body away to the hospital." That's when Peter had a glimpse of Heaven. He said, "I looked around myself and I saw an incredibly beautiful *bright loving white light* above me. I wanted to go to that white light more than anything" (emphasis added). Pause there for a moment.

Have you ever heard someone refer to light as being "loving"?

His choice of words is quite interesting, isn't it?

Could such a description indicate that he was in the presence of Jesus?

Sellers continues, "I've never wanted anything more." Again, that's quite a statement coming from someone who owned more than 80 classic cars. Sellers's personal collection included a Ferrari, a Maserati, and a Rolls-Royce. And yet, as desirable as these man-made works-of-art on wheels may be, they cannot satisfy the intense hunger within our hearts. Philosopher Blaise Pascal rightly observed, "There is a God-shaped vacuum in the heart of every man which cannot be filled by any created thing, but only by God the Creator, made known through Jesus Christ."[72]

For his part, Peter Sellers concluded he was in the presence of God: "I know there was love, real love, on the other side of the light which was attracting me so much. It was kind and loving and I remember thinking, 'That's God.'"[73] When I read Peter Sellers's story, I couldn't help but wonder: *Did God give him this glimpse of Heaven as an invitation to salvation?* If so, that would be entirely consistent with God's prodigal-loving heart. The Lord says, "I have loved you with an everlasting love; I have drawn you with unfailing kindness" (Jeremiah 31:3 NIV).

I'm not surprised that, in the wake of his encounter with the Divine, something changed within Sellers's thinking about his spiritual standing. According to those closest to him, "The experience of resurrection intensified Sellers's spiritual concern and friends discerned the start of a new introspectiveness, a sense of his not 'being there' in spirit, though present in body."[74] Sellers continued to have extended conversations with a "neighboring vicar in London, the Rev. John Hester, 'to try to reconcile the world of plenty he inhabited with the emptiness of soul that oppressed him.'"[75]

I wanted to go to that light more than anything.

This oppressive "emptiness of the soul" Sellers struggled with reminds me of what C. S. Lewis said about our unsuccessful attempts to fill the void within. Lewis writes, "If I find in myself a desire which no experience in this world can satisfy, the most probable explanation is that I was made for another world."[76] The Good News is that we no longer have to walk around with a hole in our soul. The Good Shepherd stands at the door of our heart and knocks. This good and compassionate God knows that we, His restless sheep, are lost and need to be rescued. David, the shepherd boy turned king, sang of God's relentless pursuit of His lost sheep, saying, "Your beauty and love chase after me every day of my life" (Psalm 23:6 MSG).

I love the fact that God doesn't just "chase" after you and me. He sends us a royal invitation signed and sealed with the priceless blood of Jesus. Yes, this Jesus invites us to linger with Him for all of eternity at the wedding feast in Heaven (Matthew 22:1–14). His invitation is valid whether you're young or old, rich or poor, powerful or oppressed, a film star or a janitor—or a thief, like the one to whom Jesus said, "Today you shall be with me in Paradise" (Luke 23:43). Or, as John Newton, author of the classic hymn "Amazing Grace," said on his death bed, "I am still in the land of the dying; I shall be in the land of the living soon."[77] What a glorious hope!

As I said at the outset of this book, Heaven is a place more joyful, more glorious, and more dazzling than anything you and I can imagine. Yes, Heaven is a place God has prepared for me and for *you*.

BIBLICAL VISIONS OF HEAVEN

Revelation Chapter 21 NKJV

The Apostle John wrote the book of Revelation while incarcerated in a Roman prison for preaching about Jesus. Faithful to the Lord until the end of his life, John was more than 90 years old at the time of this writing. Although he was physically in jail, his spirit was set free by God to see and to record this glimpse of Heaven.

Now I saw a new heaven and a new earth, for the first heaven and the first earth had passed away. Also there was no more sea. Then I, John, saw the holy city, New Jerusalem, coming down out of heaven from God, prepared as a bride adorned for her husband. And I heard a loud voice from heaven saying, "Behold, the tabernacle of God is with men, and He will dwell with them, and they shall be His people. God Himself will be with them and be their God. And God will wipe away every tear from their eyes; there shall be no more death, nor sorrow, nor crying. There shall be no more pain, for the former things have passed away."

Then He who sat on the throne said, "Behold, I make all things new." And He said to me, "Write, for these words are true and faithful."

And He said to me, "It is done! I am the Alpha and the Omega, the Beginning and the End. I will give of the fountain of the water of life freely to him who thirsts. He who overcomes shall inherit all things, and I will be his God and he shall be My son. But the cowardly, unbelieving, abominable, murderers, sexually immoral, sorcerers, idolaters, and all liars shall have their part in the lake which burns with fire and brimstone, which is the second death."

Then one of the seven angels who had the seven bowls filled with the seven last plagues came to me and talked with me, saying, "Come, I will show you the bride, the Lamb's wife." And he carried me away in the Spirit to a great and high mountain, and showed me the great city, the holy Jerusalem, descending out of heaven from God, having the glory of God. Her light was like a most precious stone, like a jasper stone, clear as crystal. Also she had a great and high wall with twelve gates, and twelve angels at the gates, and names written on them, which are the names of the twelve tribes of the children of Israel: three gates on the east, three gates on the north, three gates on the south, and three gates on the west.

Now the wall of the city had twelve foundations, and on them were the names of the twelve apostles of the Lamb. And he who talked with me had a gold reed to measure the city, its gates, and its wall. The city is laid out as a square; its length is as great as its breadth. And he measured the city with the reed: twelve thousand furlongs. Its length, breadth, and height are equal. Then he measured its wall: one hundred and forty-four cubits, according to the measure of a man, that is, of an angel. The construction of its wall was of jasper; and the city was pure gold, like clear glass. The foundations of the wall of the city were adorned with all kinds of precious stones: the first foundation was jasper, the second sapphire, the third chalcedony, the fourth emerald, the fifth sardonyx, the sixth sardius, the seventh chrysolite, the eighth beryl, the ninth topaz, the tenth chrysoprase, the eleventh jacinth, and the twelfth amethyst.

The twelve gates were twelve pearls: each individual gate was of one pearl. And the street of the city was pure gold, like transparent glass.

But I saw no temple in it, for the Lord God Almighty and the Lamb are its temple. The city had no need of the sun or of the moon to shine in it, for the glory of God illuminated it. The Lamb is its light. And the nations of those who are saved shall walk in its light, and the kings of the earth bring their glory and honor into it. Its gates shall not be shut at all by day (there shall be no night there). And they shall bring the glory and the honor of the nations into it. But there shall by no means enter it anything that defiles, or causes an abomination or a lie, but only those who are written in the Lamb's Book of Life.

Genesis 28:10–17 NKJV

Jacob was blessed by God in so many ways, but lived his life without a vision of his place in God's story. While sleeping under the stars, God appeared to Jacob and revealed some startling news: God's blessing on him would extend to countless generations to come.

Now Jacob went out from Beersheba and went toward Haran. So he came to a certain place and stayed there all night, because the sun had set. And he took one of the stones of that place and put it at his head, and he lay down in that place to sleep. Then he dreamed, and behold, a ladder was set up on the earth, and its top reached to heaven; and there the angels of God were ascending and descending on it.

And behold, the LORD stood above it and said: "I am the LORD God of Abraham your father and the God of Isaac; the land on which you lie I will give to you and your descendants. Also your descendants shall be as the dust of the earth; you shall spread abroad to the west and the east, to the north and the south; and in you and in your seed all the families of the earth shall be blessed. Behold, I am with you and will keep you wherever you go, and will bring you back to this land; for I will not leave you until I have done what I have spoken to you."

Then Jacob awoke from his sleep and said, "Surely the LORD is in this place, and I did not know it." And he was afraid and said, "How awesome is this place! This is none other than the house of God, and this is the gate of heaven!"

Acts 7:54–56 NKJV

The first martyr of the Christian Church is Stephen. In the moment before his death by stoning he is given a glimpse of Heaven.

When they heard these things they were cut to the heart, and they gnashed at him with their teeth. But he, being full of the Holy Spirit, gazed into heaven and saw the glory of God, and Jesus standing at the right hand of God, and said, "Look! I see the heavens opened and the Son of Man standing at the right hand of God!"

Matthew 3:13–17 NKJV

Jesus approached his cousin John the Baptist to be baptized at the start of His public ministry. In that sacred moment, we're given a glimpse of the eternal fellowship of the Trinity—Jesus the Son of God who was baptized, the Holy Spirit of God which descended upon Him as a dove, and God the Father who spoke from Heaven.

Then Jesus came from Galilee to John at the Jordan to be baptized by him. And John tried to prevent Him, saying, "I need to be baptized by You, and are You coming to me?"

But Jesus answered and said to him, "Permit it to be so now, for thus it is fitting for us to fulfill all righteousness." Then he allowed Him.

When He had been baptized, Jesus came up immediately from the water; and behold, the heavens were opened to Him, and He saw the Spirit of God descending like a dove and alighting upon Him. And suddenly a voice came from heaven, saying, "This is My beloved Son, in whom I am well pleased."

ENDNOTES

1–John MacArthur, *The Glory of Heaven: The Truth About Heaven, Angels, and Eternal Life* (Wheaton, IL: Crossway, 2013), 15.

2–Ibid., 16.

3– Mark Galli, "Incredible Journeys: What to Make of Visits to Heaven," *Christianity Today*, accessed 12/12/13, http://www.christianitytoday.com/ct/2012/december/incredible-journeys.html?paging=off.

4–Charles H. Spurgeon, quoted in Paul Lee Tan, *Encyclopedia of 7700 Illustrations* (Garland, TX: Bible Communications, 1996).

5–Rick Warren, *The Purpose Driven Life: What on Earth Am I Here For?* (Grand Rapids, MI: Zondervan, 2012).

6–Eben Alexander, M.D., *Proof of Heaven* (New York, NY: Simon & Schuster, 2012), 8–9.

7–Randy Alcorn, *TouchPoints: Heaven* (Carol Stream, IL: Tyndale House, 2008), 124.

8–Alexander, *Proof of Heaven*, 34.

9–Ibid., 24.

10–Ibid., 8.

11–Ibid., 9.

12–Ibid.

13–Ibid., 157.

14–Ibid., 83.

15–Ibid., 160.

16–Ibid., 96.

17–J.C. Ryle, *Heaven* (Ross-shire, UK: Christian Focus Publications, 2000), 84.

18–"List of Motor Vehicle Deaths in U.S. by Year," Wikipedia.org, accessed 12/16/2013, http://en.wikipedia.org/wiki/List_of_motor_vehicle_deaths_in_U.S._by_year.

19–Don Piper, *90 Minutes in Heaven* (Grand Rapids, MI: Revell, 2004), 29.

20–Ibid., 26.

21–Ibid., 31.

22–Ibid., 29.

23–*"Walter Savage Landor Quotes,"* Quotes.net, STANDS4 LLC, 2013, accessed 12/18/2013, http://www.quotes.net/quote/3103.

24–Piper, *90 Minutes in Heaven*, 34–35.

25–Ibid., 35.

26–Richard Kent and Val Fotherby, *Final Frontier* (Grand Rapids, MI: Zondervan, 1997).

27–Kevin and Alex Malarkey, *The Boy Who Came Back from Heaven: A Remarkable Account of Miracles, Angels, and Life Beyond This World* (Carol Stream, IL: Tyndale House Publishers, Inc., 2010), 50.

28–Billy Graham, *Angels* (Nashville, TN: Thomas Nelson, 1995), 32.

29–"Stephen Hawking Says 'No God; Heaven Is a Fairy Tale'—Twitter Lights Up," *Examiner.com*, 5/16/2011, http://www.examiner.com/article/stephen-hawking-says-no-god-heaven-is-a-fairy-tale-twitter-lights-up.

30–"Q&A with Mary C. Neal, MD," Amazon.com, accessed 12/19/2013, http://www.amazon.com/To-Heaven-Back-Doctors-Extraordinary/dp/0307731715/ref=sr_1_2?ie=UTF8&qid=1387166746&sr=8-2&keywords=Flight+to+Heaven.

31–"To Heaven and Back: Cynic finds God in near-death experience," *TODAY* show, 7/19/2012, accessed 12/19/2013, http://www.today.com/id/48229151/#.UrO8UY0ma6E.

32–Mary Neal, *To Heaven and Back: A Doctor's Extraordinary Account of Her Death, Heaven, Angels, and Life Again* (Waterbrook Press), 116.

33–Raymond A. Moody, Jr. MD, *The Light Beyond: New Explorations by the author of Life After Life* (New York, NY: Bantam Books, 1988), 12.

34–Crystal McVea and Alex Tresniowski, *Waking Up in Heaven* (New York, NY: Howard Books, 2013).

35–Ibid.

36–Joni Eareckson Tada, *Heaven: Your Real Home* (Grand Rapids, MI: Zondervan, 1996), 67.

37–Rebecca Ruter Springer, *My Dream of Heaven: A Nineteenth-Century Spiritual Classic* (Tulsa, OK: Harrison House, 2002), vii.

38–Ibid., 6–7.

39—Ibid., 9.

40—Billy Graham, *The Enduring Classics of Billy Graham: The Secret of Happiness, Hope for the Troubled Heart, Death and the Life After* (Nashville, TN: Thomas Nelson, 2002).

41—J. Vernon McGee, *Death of a Little Child* (Pasadena, CA: Thru the Bible Radio, July 1970), 20.

42—Randy Alcorn, *Heaven* (Carol Stream, IL: Tyndale House, 2004), 290.

43—Ibid., 341.

44—Todd Burpo, *Heaven Is for Real* (Nashville, TN: Thomas Nelson, 2010), 94–96.

45—Charles H. Spurgeon, "Infant Salvation," Sermon 411, September 29, 1861, www.spurgeongems.org.

46—Alcorn, *Heaven*, 394–395.

47—"Inspirational Quotes in Digital Form via Pinterest!" My Starbucks Idea, 8/9/2012, accessed 1/2/2014, http://blogs.starbucks.com/blogs/customer/archive/2012/06/08/the-quotes-on-cups-are-back-in-digital-form-via-pinterest.aspx.

48—"Heaven, Hell, & Rewards: Part 2," Ken Boa, *KenBoa.org*, accessed 1/3/2014, https://www.kenboa.org/text_resources/teaching_letters/kens_teaching_letter/2103.

49—Joey Green, *Philosophy on the Go* (Philadelphia, PA: Running Press Book Publishers, 2007), 222.

50—John Eldredge, *The Journey of Desire* (Nashville, TN: Thomas Nelson, 2000), 111.

51—Piper, *90 Minutes in Heaven*, 29.

52—Alexander, *Proof of Heaven*, 9.

53—Alexander, *Proof of Heaven*, 46.

54—Jeffrey Long, MD, *Evidence of the Afterlife: The Science of Near-Death Experiences* (New York, NY: HarperOne, 2010), 3.

55—Ibid., 58.

56—P. M. H. Atwater, *Beyond the Light* (New York, NY: Birch Lane Press, 1994), 49.

57—Alcorn, *Heaven*, 394–395.

58—Brennan Manning, *The Ragamuffin Gospel* (Sisters, OR: Multnomah Publishers, Inc., 2005), 25.

59—George Gallup Jr. *Adventures in Immortality* (New York: Mcgraw-Hill, 1982), 1.

60–Kent and Fotherby, *The Final Frontier* (Grand Rapids, MI: Zondervan, 1997).

61–Ibid.

62–Petti Wagner, *Murdered Heiress: Living Witness* (Shippensburg, PA: Acts Publishing, 1984), 66, 67.

63–Alexander, *Proof of Heaven*, 95.

64–Manning, *The Ragamuffin Gospel*, 104.

65–Eareckson Tada, *Heaven: Your Real Home,* 34.

66–Charles H. Spurgeon, *Morning and Evening* (Blacksburg, VA: Wilder Publications, 2008), 173.

67–Richard Gray, "There could be 100 billion Earth-like planets say astronomers," *The Telegraph*, April 3, 2013, http://www.telegraph.co.uk/science/space/9969746/There-could-be-100-billion-Earth-like-planets-say-astronomers.html.

68–Spurgeon, *Morning and Evening*, 172–173.

69–Alcorn, *Heaven*, 217.

70–Gloria Gaither, *Something Beautiful: The Stories Behind a Half-Century of the Songs of Bill and Gloria Gather* (New York, NY: FaithWords, 2007), 19.

71–Max Lucado, *Experiencing the Heart of Jesus Workbook* (Nashville, TN: Thomas Nelson Publishers, 2003).

72–"The Secret That Will Change Your Life," Chris Lutes, ChristianityToday.com, accessed 1/9/2014, http://www.christianitytoday.com/iyf/hottopics/faithvalues/8c6030.html.

73–Lee Bailey, *The Near-Death Experience: A Reader* (New York, NY: Routledge, 1996), 73–74.

74–Ibid., 74.

75–Ibid.

76–C. S. Lewis, *Mere Christianity* (New York: HarperCollins, 2001), 136.

77–Billy Graham, *Nearing Home: Life, Faith, and Finishing Well* (Nashville, TN: Thomas Nelson Publishers, 2011), 93.

ABOUT THE AUTHOR

Bob DeMoss has authored 26 books including five *New York Times* bestsellers, served as an associate publisher at HarperCollins Christian Publishing, and founded Focus on the Family's *PluggedIN* magazine. He and his family live in Franklin, Tennessee.

Don't miss the inspiring music CD featuring classic hits from great Christian artists like: Mercy Me, Paul Baloche, Christy Nockels, New Life Worship, Darlene Zschech, and many more.

To learn more visit:
www.worthypublishing.com/Heaven